The
Know It All
Book of
Education

Waldo Rochow, MBA

Published by the author
Edited by Will Rochow
Cover by Waldo Rochow
>   with elements of *The portal* by: pualv (www.flickr.com/photos/8460740@N05)
>   CC-BY 2.0 (accessed: 27 Jul 2014)

Website: http:// know-it-all.rochow.info

ISBN: 978-0-9938812-8-2

Volume #08 in the *Know It All* series:

To my loving wife Joanne, for putting up
with my silly side all these years;

To my sons Karl and Paul, for following in
my silly shoes;

To my parents, for instilling in all your kids
and grandkids an appreciation for the silly
side of life;

To my brother Will, for your tireless editing
support; and

To all the people of the world, for giving me
something to laugh about.

Thank you for joining me on this journey. The purpose of this book is actually deeper than its tongue-in-cheek treatment here suggests. While on the surface it might appear that I am scoffing at higher learning, nothing could be further from the truth. It is my goal to encourage the reader to think, and study, and to not be satisfied with the status quo. In fact, I would be thrilled if you fill this book with your own observations.

As someone with an interest in this subject, why shouldn't you write *The Book of Knowledge*? You just might be seen by future generations as the *Father* or *Mother* of the study of Education. Sure, you won't be the first author on the subject (after all, neither was I), but you could be the most significant.

I hope that you will become a contagion of inquisitiveness. Be that gal or that guy that is constantly asking *why*. Contaminate your friends and family with curiosity. Consider the possibility that much, if not all, that we know today on any subject may be completely wrong. Challenge the assumptions upon which your knowledge is based.

You just might be surprised what you can still learn after you *know it all*.

-- Waldo Rochow, MBA

www.ingramcontent.com/pod-product-compliance
Lightning Source LLC
Chambersburg PA
CBHW070956040426
42443CB00007B/527